CW01467799

Mexican Cooking

THE FIRST
MEXICAN-AMERICAN
COOKBOOK

APPLEWOOD BOOKS
Bedford, Massachusetts

Although an exact date has not been established, *Mexican Cooking* was first published around 1908 by the Gebhardt Chili Powder Company of San Antonio, Texas.

Thank you for purchasing an Applewood book. Applewood reprints America's lively classics—books from the past that are still of interest to modern readers.

For a free copy of our
current catalog, write to:
Applewood Books
P.O. Box 365
Bedford, MA 01730

ISBN 1-55709-473-X

1 3 5 7 9 10 8 6 4 2

This cookbook has been reprinted in cooperation with the Culinary Trust, which is the philanthropic arm of the International Association of Culinary Professionals (IACP). The Trust celebrates the culinary past and future by funding educational and charitable programs related to the culinary industry (including scholarships for students and career professionals; library research and travel grants for food writers), cookbook preservation and restoration; and hunger alleviation. Tax-deductible gifts to the Culinary Trust should be sent to:

The Culinary Trust
304 West Liberty Street, Suite 201,
Louisville, KY 40202
Website: www.theculinarytrust.com
Phone: (502) 581-9786 x264

FOREWORD

The Gebhardt Chili Powder
Company was founded by
William Gebhardt, a German,
who migrated about 1885 to
New Braunfels, Texas. Gebhardt
opened a café, which served
chilis imported from Mexico.
To preserve them, he dried and
crushed them into powder. He
began bottling his powder, and
in 1890, he opened a factory in
San Antonio. Six years later
he trademarked the name
"Gebhardt's Eagle Brand Chili
Powder."

The powder became an important ingredient to such an extent

that recipes in Texas cookbooks specifically recommended its use.

When Gebhardt began marketing chili powder to a wider audience beyond Texas, he ran into a very serious problem—consumers not familiar with Tex-Mex cookery had little idea what to do with it. To help cooks understand Tex-Mex cookery, Gebhardt produced a small 32-page cookery pamphlet. This cookbooklet was originally published about 1908. As such, it was the first English-language booklet published in the United States that focused on Mexican-American cookery. It proved so successful that new editions of it were regularly published through the 1950s.

In 1911, Gebhardt sold his company to his brothers-in-law, who expanded their product line to include beans and tamales. During the 1920s, they introduced to the tourist trade Gebhardt's Original Mexican Dinner Package, consisting of cans of chili con carne, Mexican Style Beans, shuck-wrapped Tamales, Deviled Chili Meat, and a bottle of Chili Powder —all for one dollar. By the 1930s, Gebhardt products were sold throughout the United States and Mexico. The company survived until 1960 when it was purchased by Beatrice Foods, which in turn was acquired by ConAgra in 1990.

—Andrew F. Smith

Mexican Cooking

To the American Housekeeper

A CHANGE of Menu is one of the constantly recurring and vexing problems of the day. "What shall I have for dinner?" is a source of never-ending worry.

In presenting to the American housekeeper the first MEXICAN COOK BOOK ever printed, we have spared neither labor nor expense in our efforts to give dishes that are pleasing, novel and easily prepared.

While of the most simple nature, these recipes are those used by some of the most famous chefs of Old Mexico, and a careful reading of the following pages will enable you to surprise and please your friends and family with dishes that have graced the table of President Diaz and have made Mexican cooks as famous as those of France.

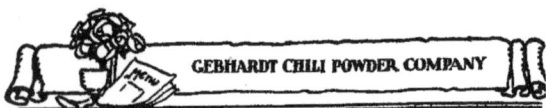

Gebhardt's Eagle Chili Powder

MEXICAN dishes have long been noted for a peculiar piquancy; an illusive flavor, as pleasing as it was hard to reproduce. Few but the native-born ever learned the art of properly preparing and blending the various spices needed to give *That Real Mexican Tang*.

Even when the knowledge was acquired, the difficulty of securing and preparing the necessary ingredients made the famous dishes of Mexico an impossibility in the average home, and it was not until the *Gebhardt Chili Powder Company* succeeded in preparing these spices and blending them into the perfection found only in *Eagle Chili Powder* that Mexican dishes really became practical.

Since then the growing popularity in the United States of Mexican cookery has been remarkable, and to-day *Chili Con Carne, Tamales, Huevos Con Chili*, and dozens of other dishes are as common in many American homes as our traditional beefsteak.

In the manufacture of *Gebhardt's Eagle Chili Powder*, only genuine Mexican chili-pepper, grown especially for this purpose on our own Haciendas in Mexico, are used— in fact, it is the only preparation in which Mexican chilis are used exclusively. Perfectly blended with the chili are the purest and most select of the spices used in every Mexican household, and it is largely due to the use of this chili and spices that the Mexican people owe their wonderful digestion and their consequent longevity.

The users of *Gebhardt's Eagle Chili Powder* will find it not only a delightful seasoning

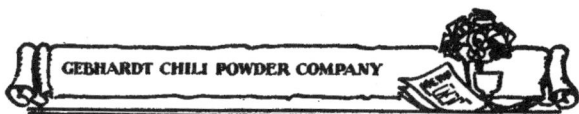

for all kinds of meats and soups, but healthful in every way.

Gebhardt's Eagle Chili Powder is accepted by the United States Government as the standard for chili powders, being adopted by the commissary departments of both the army and navy, and is the one preparation of this character that has ever received such an endorsement.

A Word of Caution

The success of *Gebhardt's Eagle Chili Powder* has naturally brought forth a host of spurious chili powders or compounds, of which the public should beware, as they are generally composed of common hot peppers, adulterations and more or less poisonous coloring matter, and entirely devoid of the vegetable oil to which the Mexican Chili Pepper owes its flavor.

When other peppers are substituted for Mexican chili, the preparation lacks in oil and is so dry that it may be shaken like salt or pepper from a shaker; whereas, the oil in the genuine Mexican chili causes the powder to pack tight in the bottle. It is to this oil that chili pepper owes its flavor, and for this reason *Gebhardt's Eagle Chili Powder* is the only preparation giving *That Real Mexican Tang.*

Gebhardt's Eagle Chili Con Carne

WHILE Chili Con Carne may be easily prepared from any of the recipes given in this book, those who prefer it ready to serve will find in *Eagle Brand* a dish that possesses *That Real Mexican Tang,* usually found only in the most exclusive homes and best cafés of old Mexico; a dish in which the discriminating housekeeper will be quick to

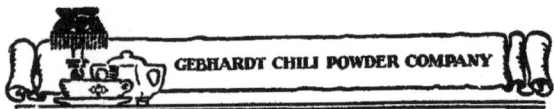

appreciate the unusual quality of the meat and the peculiarly piquant flavor of the spices—the same spices that have made *Gebhardt's Chili Powder* the accepted standard of all chili preparations.

Until you have used *Eagle Brand* you have never tasted a genuine ready-prepared Chili Con Carne. We do not believe you have ever tasted a Mexican dish where the chili spices were so perfectly blended with rich, firm, wholesome meat.

Prepared in what noted experts declare to be the cleanest and most thoroughly sanitary kitchens ever built for this purpose, with every operation directly under the eye of Pure Food inspectors, we do not hesitate to say that *Eagle Chili Con Carne* is as clean, wholesome, and as full-flavored as you could prepare in your own home, if you had the best markets of old Mexico to draw from.

Proper cooking is no less important than the selection of the ingredients and, in order that every package of *Eagle Chili Con Carne* may receive just the right flavor, each step of its preparation is under the direct supervision of trained Mexican carne cooks, whose years of experience in blending the spices used in *Gebhardt's Eagle Chili Powder* enable them to offer a dish that is a pleasant surprise to the jaded appetite.

Prepared with rare skill and with the one thought—make the best—*Gebhardt's Eagle Chili Con Carne* costs but a trifle more than the ordinary kind, yet is twice as economical because it goes twice as far; every package is solid meat with just enough genuine Mexican frijoles to give it the proper nutty flavor, every atom of it is appetizing and nourishing.

4

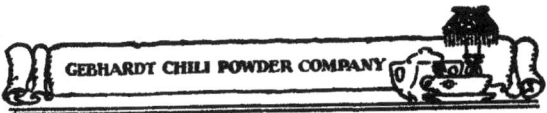

Gebhardt's Eagle Tabasco Sauce

FEW people realize the necessity of spices in our every-day foods, but if one will only attempt to imagine a soup, roast, or in fact, anything we eat without salt, pepper, etc., they will quickly understand the absolute necessity of proper seasoning.

Spices of the pepper variety are really more important than any other, for while the body contains a certain amount of salt, the pepper which digestion demands and without which perfect digestion is impossible, must be taken into the system.

There is no more delightful way of doing it than through the use of *Gebhardt's Eagle Tabasco Sauce*. With this article the ingenious cook will prepare hundreds of dishes in a new and appetizing way. It imparts a delightful relish and exquisite flavor to meats, soups, fish, gravies, etc., and is a material aid to good digestion. A few drops are all that are necessary.

In the manufacture of *Gebhardt's Eagle Tabasco Sauce* we use only the pure extract of the finest tabasco peppers, which are grown especially for us in the State of Tabasco, Mexico. These are treated in the most thoroughly scientific manner and the result is a sauce par-excellence.

Gebhardt's Eagle Tabasco Sauce does not contain either artificial coloring or preserving matter; it is the pure extract of the best Tabasco peppers. It is highly concentrated and should always be mixed with gravies or a drop or two sprinkled on meats, soups, etc. An oyster cocktail is incomplete without the addition of a few drops of *Gebhardt's Eagle Tabasco Sauce*.

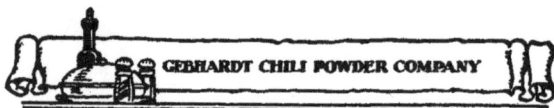

Recipes
Para la Preparacion de Carnes
Meat Recipes

Gebhardt's Eagle (Standard) Chili Con Carne

Cut two pounds of beef into one-half inch squares, add about two ounces chopped tallow, then salt it. Use a high pot (granite-ware is best), heat in this pot two tablespoonsful of lard; add to this a small-sized chopped onion; when the onion is about half done, add the meat; stir well until the meat is separated and white, then let steam or parboil (with cover off) over a rather hot fire, stirring frequently until the juice of the meat is boiled down, and when it starts to fry add about one and one-half pints of hot water, three table-spoonsful of *Gebhardt's Eagle Chili Powder* and a few buttons of chopped garlic; stir well and let simmer until meat is tender.

Chili Con Carne, ó Azado Al Estilo Mexicano—
Real Mexican Chili Con Carne; also called Azado

Take two pounds of meat, cut in small pieces and put in a frying-pan where three tablespoonsful of lard have been heated, cooking until slightly brown. Have ready two buttons of chopped garlic, salt and pepper to taste, a medium-sized onion cut into small pieces, a ripe tomato cut in small slices (or six to ten mashed green tomatoes well mixed with a little water.)

First add garlic and onion to the meat, let cook for twenty or thirty minutes and add tomatoes, salt and pepper and two tablespoonsful of *Gebhardt's Eagle Chili Powder*, mixing thoroughly with one-half cupful of hot water, let boil until meat is very tender; add additional hot water as needed.

This chili should be made with considerable gravy, especially where

6

green tomatoes are used. If desired one-half teaspoonful of sugar and one teaspoonful of vinegar may be added fifteen or twenty minutes before the chili is done, giving the dish a most delightful flavor.

Chili Con Carne Americano—*American Chili Con Carne*

To one pound of meat cut into small pieces add one-quarter pound of lard or grease and simmer in a covered vessel until half done. Then add one quart of hot water, one tablespoonful or more of salt and from one to two tablespoonsful of *Gebhardt's Eagle Chili Powder* and boil slowly until meat is tender. Water should be added from time to time to make up for the loss by evaporation; browned flour may be added to thicken the gravy if desired. Stir thoroughly while the chili powder is being added. One to two buttons of finely chopped garlic may be added. Serve hot.

Chili Con Carne—*Meat with Chili*

Cut or chop into small dices two pounds of beef, add a little chopped tallow and salt; place the above in a covered pot in which you have previously heated two or more tablespoonsful of lard, and steam until about half done; now add two quarts of hot water and one or two tablespoonsful of *Gebhardt's Eagle Chili Powder* according to strength desired; stir well, then boil slowly until meat is tender.

Chili Con Carne de Carnes Frias—*Meat with Chili from Cold Meats*

Wholesome Chili Con Carne may be prepared from meats left over from previous meals, such as steaks, roasts, etc. Chop the meat fine, add finely chopped onions and salt; place in a pan in which you have heated a quantity of lard and cook ten minutes; then add enough hot water to make a sauce, and a tablespoonful of *Gebhardt's Eagle Chili Powder* for each quart of the above; add flour to thicken gravy.

In any of the above, chicken may be substituted for other meat and gives the dish a much more delicate flavor.

Frijoles

Mexican Bayo or California Pink Beans are soaked over night in water; remove the old and add fresh

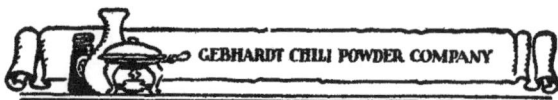

water, also a few slices of bacon, cook slowly until done, then add salt and some *Gebhardt's Eagle Chili Powder*, according to taste. Served separate or with Chili Con Carne.

Tamales

Gebhardt's Eagle (Standard) Tamales

To prepare the Corn Shucks: Cut or chop off each end of the shuck; open up and clean it of hairs or silk; put into water and soak for about one hour; separate and size them; they should be about six or seven inches long and two or two and one-half inches wide.

To prepare the Meat: Put into a one-gallon pot one pound of beef and one pound of pork (you may also put in a soup-bone); add water to the top, salt, a few buttons of garlic and a medium-sized onion cut into quarters; just fry the juice out of the onion and garlic and then remove them. Now add the meat and fry for five minutes, stirring continuously, then add about half-pint of the broth in which the meat was cooked, four tablespoonsful of *Gebhardt's Eagle Chili Powder* and salt to taste; cook about ten minutes longer, stirring all the time, then add flour enough to thicken.

Preparation of the Dough: Tamale dough is made from corn similar to hominy ground fine and is placed on the market in a dry form under various names, but if unobtainable, scalded cornmeal may be used. To two quarts of meal add broth enough to make a thick dough, half-pound of hot rendered tallow, plenty of salt and a teaspoonful of *Gebhardt's Eagle Chili Powder*, mix together and add more broth until the dough is rather thin.

To prepare the Tamales: Put a layer of dough on the husk about four inches long, one and one-half inches wide, and one-eighth inch thick; along the center spread one teaspoonful of the prepared meat; roll the whole like a cigarette and fold the small end of the husk; place them with the folded end down in a potato-strainer; place the strainer in a pot over water, cover the whole with cloth and steam for two hours; always serve hot. The above will make about one hundred tamales.

*   *   *   *   *   *   *   *   *

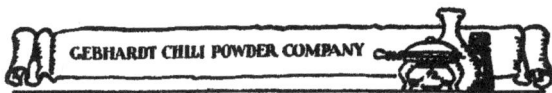

Hechos De Carne de Puerco, Gallina ó Guajolote
—Made from Pork, Chicken, or Turkey.

Preparation of Meat: Put one pound of pork, chicken, or turkey, to boil with a little salt and one button of garlic. After it is cooked, chop fine. Take three tablespoonsful of lard, put it in a frying-pan and add the meat when the lard is hot and mix with it a tablespoonful of *Gebhardt's Eagle Chili Powder* that has first been thoroughly mixed with a pinch of salt and a little hot water. Stir well, cover dish, and steam for about fifteen or twenty minutes. Sometimes raisins and pecans are added to this just before done, giving it a sweet taste. Balance of tamale is prepared same as in recipe above for *Gebhardt's Eagle Tamales.*

Tamales de Caserola—
Tamales de Caseul—*Corn Meal Pot Pie*

Cut into small slices about one pound of pork or chicken (or both mixed), add a little salt and boil until tender.

To one quart of Nixtamal or scalded cornmeal, add salt and four tablespoonsful of butter; stir into this a handful of flour and two beaten eggs, and into this pour enough broth to make a batter.

Take half a can of tomatoes, add a little butter and one tablespoonful of *Gebhardt's Eagle Chili Powder* and cook until well done; add this to the meat and mix well. Line pie-pans with the meal mixture, put in the meat, mix into layers as for chicken pie, bake very slowly and baste frequently with butter until done.

Hogaza de Ternera ó Rés—*Veal or Beef Loaf*

Use two pounds of finely chopped beef or veal and about one-half pound of pork, one tablespoonful of lard, one onion, one cupful of cracker crumbs, one teaspoonful of black pepper, two well-beaten eggs, one teaspoonful of salt, and one tablespoonful of *Gebhardt's Eagle Chili Powder.* Mix thoroughly and make into one loaf and put in a pan with one pint of water, mixed with tablespoonful of lard or butter and

9

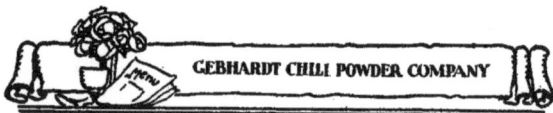

one teaspoonful of *Gebhardt's Eagle Chili Powder;* bake from one hour to one hour and a half, basting occasionally. May be served hot or cold.

Alvondigas Mexicanas—*Mexican Meat Balls*

Take equal parts of boiled beef and pork, say one pound; chop fine; add salt, a small piece of soaked bread, one egg well beaten and one teaspoonful of *Gebhardt's Eagle Chili Powder;* mix thoroughly and make into balls, putting in each a piece of hard-boiled egg; in a dish of hot lard or butter put five or six crushed tomatoes, a little chopped onion, broth, salt, and *Gebhardt's Eagle Chili Powder:* let boil a few moments and then put in the balls; when the meat is cooked it is ready for serving.

Tajadas de Rés y Ostras—*Beefsteak and Oysters*

Broil a very thick steak fifteen minutes. Put some oysters in a hot pan without any broth, stir over the fire briskly a few minutes, salt the steak and sprinkle with *Gebhardt's Eagle Chili Powder* (not too strong), then cover the steak with the oysters; bake in hot oven fifteen minutes. Remove the platter, keeping the oysters on top of the steak.

Chorizo Con Chili—*Hamburg Steak or Chili Sausage*

Grind the meat very coarse and add to each pound of meat one and one-half tablespoonsful of *Gebhardt's Eagle Chili Powder,* one button of finely chopped garlic and salt. Then add a little high grade vinegar. Mix and let stand over night. Grind again the next morning, after which it can be either fried or broiled as desired.

Guisado de Chili — *Chili Stew*

Cut two pounds of beef in slices, salt it and place in a pot in which you have heated two tablespoonsful of lard; add one medium-sized chopped onion and stew about thirty minutes; now add one quart of warm water, one-half pint canned or two large mashed tomatoes, four sliced Irish

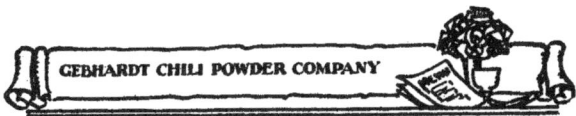

potatoes and one tablespoonful of *Gebhardt's Eagle Chili Powder*, and cook slowly until done.

Picadillo—*Mexican Hash*

Boil one-half pound of meat and chop fine as for hash, then take one tomato and one or two buttons of garlic and chop fine. Put tomato and garlic in a frying-pan, let cook for a few minutes, then add the meat and one-half teaspoonful of *Gebhardt's Eagle Chili Powder* and one onion cut fine, stirring well, and salt and pepper to suit taste. Then add broth in which meat has been boiled and boil or steam for about twenty minutes.

Goulash Americano—*American Goulash*

Cut into small squares one pound of beef, add chopped tallow, salt and one tablespoonful of *Gebhardt's Eagle Chili Powder* and mix the whole. Now put into graniteware pot two tablespoonsful of butter, melt, and when brown add four or five slices of bacon and two or three finely sliced onions; cover the pot and let fry until the onions and bacon commence to brown; then add the meat and let cook about ten minutes, stirring frequently. Now add one pint of hot water and one button of chopped garlic and let cook until meat is tender. Always keep the pot covered as close as possible.

Goulash—

Put in a saucepan a large lump of butter, put on a quick fire, and when butter boils add two or three onions and three or four slices of bacon, cover the pan carefully and let the onions and bacon get nice and brown; then take veal and cut into small pieces; put into the pan, with a little salt and a generous portion of *Gebhardt's Eagle Chili Powder*, covering the sauce pan tight. Do not put a drop of water in, but cook until tender and serve.

Higado Con Chili—*Liver with Chili*

Scrape liver fine, cut in small pieces with a sharp knife; cut up an onion fine, heat a little lard or butter in a thin frying-pan; put in liver with onions and keep stirring until done; sprinkle flour over liver; salt and

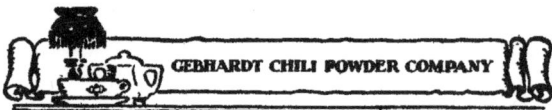

pepper; then add a tablespoonful of *Gebhardt's Eagle Chili Powder;* add water for gravy and let it boil for a few minutes, as liver easily hardens.

Riñones Con Chili—*Kidney with Chili*

Wash off the kidney and cut up fine with one medium-sized onion; have lard right hot in frying-pan; put in kidney and onion and let them fry; add salt and pepper, one bay leaf, two tablespoonsful of *Gebhardt's Eagle Chili Powder* and a little flour; lastly enough hot water for sauce, and vinegar to taste.

Chuleta de Rés—*Beef Cutlet*

Use any kind of beef not tender enough to cook quickly, cut into suitable pieces for serving, and boil just long enough to sear outside, sprinkle with salt and pepper before turning. Put in a pan with a liberal quantity of tomato sauce to which has been added a teaspoonful of *Gebhardt's Eagle Chili Powder* and cook in a moderate oven for two hours or longer. See tomato sauce recipe.

Tortas de Maíz y Carne—*Corn and Meat Croquettes*

Take cold meat of any kind, left over from previous meals, sufficient to make a quart, add a cupful of canned corn and chop or grind all fine; now add one cupful bread crumbs, salt and add *Gebhardt's Eagle Chili Powder* to taste. Mix together and if not moist enough add gravy or water and mix into cakes. Fry in hot lard.

Fricadeles de Carne Cruda—*Raw Meat Fricadels*

Cut one pound of beef into very small squares, also a medium-sized onion, mix them in hot lard and let fry. Add butter, salt and a little bay leaves, also a little cloves and allspice, one tablespoonful of *Gebhardt's Eagle Chili Powder* and a medium-sized Irish potato grated. Put in sufficient water and let boil until meat is done. A small tomato may be added and a little vinegar if liked. Before serving put in a piece of butter. This can also be made of left-over meats.

Carne de Olla—*Pot Roast*

Brown three or four pounds of rump roast in two or three tablespoonsful of lard, then add a level tea-

spoonful of salt, some black pepper and from one to two tablespoonsful of *Gebhardt's Eagle Chili Powder* and one bay leaf. Put in a casserole with one-quarter pound of carrot, a like amount of turnip and onion and two or three stalks of celery, all cut into small pieces, and add two cups of water or soup stock. Cover and cook in hot oven from three to three and one-half hours, basting every thirty minutes. Make sauce of water, flour and the juice left in the casserole, to which is added one-half teaspoonful of *Gebhardt's Eagle Chili Powder*. Pour it over the beef and serve.

Patas de Cerdo Estofadas—*Stewed Pigs' Feet*

Eight pigs' feet, one pint tomatoes, one teaspoonful chopped onion, one cupful boiling water, one bay leaf, one tablespoonful of butter, one-half tablespoonful flour, one teaspoonful of *Gebhardt's Eagle Chili Powder* Boil pigs' feet with bay leaf and salt until tender; take out bones and cut meat in small pieces; heat butter and flour, onions, tomatoes and water, cook about fifteen minutes, then add pigs' feet, season with chili powder and cook one-half hour longer.

Jamón Hervido—*Boiled Ham*

Cover the ham with warm water, let it come to a boil, put in one-half teacupful of brown sugar, one teaspoonful of *Gebhardt's Eagle Chili Powder*, set it back on the stove and keep it at a boiling point for three hours; take off the skin; put ham in a roasting-pan and cover with bread crumbs, a few cloves, and sprinkle with chili powder. Put in hot oven until brown.

Menudo—*Tripe, Mexican Style*

Take tripe after it has been well cleaned and put to boil in one quart of hot water until tender; add one or two buttons of garlic chopped fine; one or two tablespoonsful of *Gebhardt's Eagle Chili Powder*, one can of hominy; stir well and let boil until done. Serve hot.

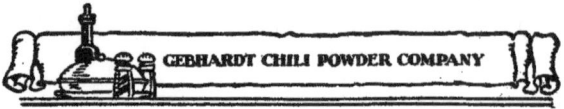

Menudo Frito Con Chili—*Tripe with Chili*

Have your tripe cooked until well done, cut in fine strips about 3 or 4 inches long; heat some lard in a frying-pan until very hot; cut up a small-sized onion fine; put strips with the hot grease, then add onions; let fry till light brown, then add two heaping teaspoonsful of *Gebhardt's Eagle Chili Powder;* let fry a few minutes longer and serve. If you desire gravy add a little hot water.

Peroskys de Tiempo Alegre—*Rag-Time Peroskys*

As one often has eggs, pie-crusts, rice and cold meats left over, this will be found a good way to utilize them: To two cupsful of finely chopped meat add one cupful of boiled rice, three hard-boiled eggs chopped fine; chop up an onion and brown in a little butter and add to the meat two raw eggs, salt to taste, one teaspoonful of *Gebhardt's Eagle Chili Powder* and mix well. Roll rich pie dough or crust thin, cut out with a small saucer, spread a spoonful of the mixture over the crust, fold and bake until brown.

Hijo de Carabina. (Vianda muy antigua de un Rural Texano)—*Son of a Gun.* (*This is an old Texas "Ranger" dish*)

Stew part of the liver, heart, sweetbreads and melts of one hog; season with salt to suit taste, and ten minutes before done add two tablespoonsful of *Gebhardt's Eagle Chili Powder*.

Pastel de Puerco de California—*California Pork Pie*

Brown thoroughly two pounds of loin of pork, which has been cut in pieces. Cover with five large cupsful of water and stew slowly until tender. Season with black pepper, salt, two rounded teaspoonsful of

Gebhardt's Eagle Chili Powder (more can be used if liked very sharp) thicken gravy very little with flour.

Make a good thick cornmeal mush, and add two well-beaten eggs; take baking-dish and put in a layer of mush; sprinkle with some chopped olives, ripe or green; add pork and gravy; cover with the rest of the mush and bake twenty minutes.

The gravy in baking draws up through the top layer of meal.

Chorizo Mexicano—*Mexican Sausage*

Take four pounds of pork and chop fine, add one head of garlic, four teacupsful of vinegar, salt to taste, and from four to six tablespoonsful of *Gebhardt's Eagle Chili Powder*. Mix thoroughly and let stand over night; then put in the sausage casing. When ready, it can be fried with eggs, added to Sopa de Arroz (rice), or baked or broiled.

Recipes de Gallina
Chicken Recipes

Gallina Frita Con Chili y Arróz—*Fried Chicken with Chili and Rice*

Cut up a spring chicken and fry in hot lard; when half done add one onion chopped fine, a green sweet pepper, one tomato, one or two tablespoonsful of *Gebhardt's Eagle Chili Powder*, one-half cupful of rice washed and dried, a pinch of salt and pepper, and enough water to allow the rice to boil until well done. Then add one bay leaf and serve.

Gallina Picada Con Arróz—*Minced Chicken with Rice*

Boil a chicken until tender; let cool off and chop fine; then wash and dry a cupful of rice and put into a suitable pot containing hot lard or butter and fry until light brown. Now add to the rice one chopped tomato, one chopped onion, one sweet green pepper cut fine, a pinch of salt and two tablespoonsful of *Gebhardt's Eagle Chili Powder*. Cook together for fifteen minutes, then mix chicken, some of the broth, rice, etc. Heat thoroughly and serve.

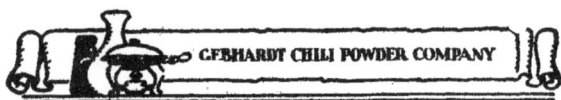

Arróz y Gallina á la Valenciana—*Rice and Chicken a la Valenciana*

Fry in hot lard to a golden brown a chicken cut in pieces. When half fried add a peeled button of garlic and onion chopped fine and from one to two table-spoonsful of *Gebhardt's Eagle Chili Powder* with a pinch of salt. With this is served rice prepared as follows: Take one cupful of rice well washed, a scant teaspoonful of salt, three cupsful of boiled water and a small spoonful of lard. The rice should be washed in cold water until all cloudiness is removed, for which five or six waters will be necessary. While washing bring to a boiling point three brimful cups of water, add a level teaspoonful of salt and a small spoonful of lard. When water is boiling add the rice and let boil from ten to fifteen minutes, keeping the cover partially over. At the end of fifteen minutes the water should be absorbed and the grains of rice soft and separated instead of the soggy mass so often seen. Remove the cover and let the rice dry in the pot for about five minutes, then place on the back of the stove and continue the drying out for about twenty or thirty minutes longer. A teaspoonful of *Gebhardt's Eagle Chili Powder* and a couple of large sweet green Spanish peppers may also be added to the rice while it is still boiling.

Fricasé de Gallina—*Fricassee of Chicken*

Unjoint a good-sized chicken, season with salt and pepper and put into a saucepan of boiling hot lard, frying to a light brown; one tablespoonful of lard will be sufficient. Remove the chicken and stir into the saucepan a sifted tablespoonful of flour; when it comes to a light brown, add a finely chopped onion and continue to stir until onion is brown; then add one table-spoonful of minced parsley; about one-half button of garlic chopped very fine and one tablespoonful of *Gebhardt's Eagle Chili Powder*, also a finely chopped tomato if desired. Return the chicken to the saucepan and let it stew together for ten minutes, after which add one and one-half pints of hot water and simmer until chicken is tender.

This dish is greatly improved by the addition of one-half can of mushrooms, or a small glass of sherry may be added just before serving.

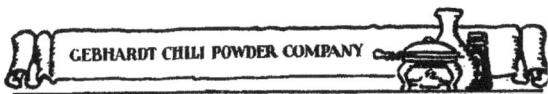

Fricasé Dorado de Gallina—*Brown Fricassee of Chicken*

Unjoint the chicken, brown in a few spoonsful of hot butter or bacon grease, then transfer to a kettle. Put in the skillet sufficient *Gebhardt's Eagle Chili Powder*, salt and sifted flour to absorb the grease, stirring it until thoroughly brown; add one pint of hot water and continue to stir until thickened, then strain over the chicken and simmer until tender.

Gallina Con Chili y Frijoles—*Chili Chicken with Frijoles*

Soak one pint of frijoles (Bayo Beans) over night; put in kettle with three quarts of cold water; boil three hours. Chop one stew chicken fine; fry brown in two tablespoonsful of hot lard or butter and when partially brown add one chopped onion; when thoroughly browned pour in a one-pound can of tomatoes and add two to three heaping tablespoonsful of *Gebhardt's Eagle Chili Powder*. Stir this mixture into the beans half an hour before serving; stir frequently and add more hot water if too thick.

Pasta de Gallina—*Chicken Pasties*

Use one cupful of chopped mushrooms to four cupful of cold minced chicken; add one and one-half cupsful of white sauce; the well-beaten yolks of two eggs; one teaspoonful of onion juice; one teaspoonful of minced parsley, salt and *Gebhardt's Eagle Chili Powder* to taste. Shape into little cakes, crumb and egg them and fry in deep hot lard.

Gallina Guisada Con Verduras—*Boiled Chicken with Vegetables*

Take one spring chicken, cut in small pieces and put in a frying-pan with three tablespoonsful of hot lard and fry until brown. Add two slices of bacon cut in small dices to a cupful of butter-beans, and boil with one can of peas, one can of tomatoes and one Irish potato sliced in small dices. Then take about two buttons of chopped garlic, salt, one-half teaspoonful

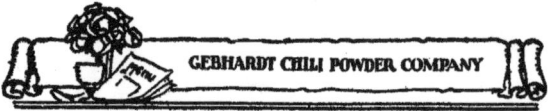

of black pepper and mix with one cupful of rice which has been boiled as directed in Chicken a la Valenciana; add with chicken in pot where beans have been boiling and in the same water, adding one tablespoonful of *Gebhardt's Eagle Chili Powder;* cover tight and let boil until done. Serve hot.

Recipes
Para Ostras, Pescado y Caza
Oysters, Fish and Game

Ostras Azadas—*Panned or Broiled Oysters*

Wash oysters quickly in cold water, drain, put in a saucepan in which you have heated one tablespoonful of butter for each one dozen oysters, add a dash of salt, black pepper and sprinkle liberally with *Gebhardt's Eagle Chili Powder,* cover and broil over a hot fire until edges curl and oysters are plump. Serve on toast.

Ostras Cocidas en Sus Conchas—*Scalloped Oysters*

Wash and drain one quart of oysters, placing them in layers in a baking-dish, using first one layer of dry bread crumbs or cracker crumbs, then a layer of oysters, sprinkled liberally with *Gebhardt's Eagle Chili Powder* and salt. When filled moisten with the oyster liquor and milk and cover with crumbs; add one tablespoonful of butter and bake for one-half hour in a slow oven.

Ostras Angeles —*Oyster Angels*

Wrap each oyster in a thin slice of half-cooked bacon, impaling with a toothpick; sprinkle with salt and

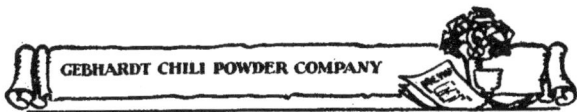

Gebhardt's Eagle Chili Powder; broil and serve on toast.

Marmelada—*Jambalaya*

One and one-half cupsful of dry boiled rice; one slice ham cut into small pieces; one finely cut large pork sausage; one level coffeespoonful *Gebhardt's Eagle Chili Powder;* one and one-half dozen oysters; one-half teaspoonful salt; one tablespoonful butter. Put oysters in a dry hot skillet to draw the water from them, take out and drain, fry the sausages and ham in butter, stir in rice, salt and chili powder; then add oysters.

This is a famous Creole dish.

Ostras Ficticias—*Mock Oysters*

Slice fine medium-sized green tomatoes. Make a batter by beating until light, yolks of two eggs, add one-quarter teacupful of sweet milk; one level teaspoonful of salt; two level teaspoonsful of *Gebhardt's Eagle Chili Powder* and enough flour to make a stiff batter. Beat whites of eggs to stiff froth and add to batter; let stand one-half hour, then beat again, then dip sliced tomatoes one at a time into batter and fry in hot drippings or butter.

Perdices—*Braised Partridges*

Clean and truss the birds, roll them in flour well seasoned with *Gebhardt's Eagle Chili Powder.* Put in the oven until partly baked, perhaps ten or fifteen minutes; cover them with chopped vegetables, cabbage, carrot, celery and turnip, and salt to taste. Set back in the oven, cover the baking-pan and cook an hour. Remove to a hot platter, the birds in the center and the vegetables in a ring around them.

Conejo Estofado—*Stewed Rabbit*

Prepare one young rabbit; cut up; add two quarts of water, one cupful of vinegar, one onion and salt to taste; boil one hour. Then add one tablespoonful of *Gebhardt's Eagle Chili Powder* and cook twenty to thirty minutes longer; thicken gravy and serve.

Holibut (Pescado) Azado ó Tajada de Holibut— *Broiled Halibut or Halibut Steak*

Cut slices of fish about one inch thick, season with salt and pepper and sprinkle liberally with *Gebhardt's*

19

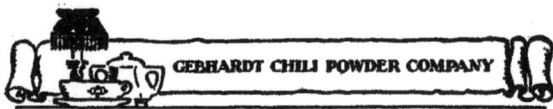

Eagle Chili Powder; then lay in melted butter for one-half hour, allowing three tablespoonful of butter to one pound of fish; roll them in flour or cracker crumbs and broil about twenty minutes, serving very hot.

Pescado Cocido al Horno Con Salsa de Tomate— *Baked Fish with Tomato Sauce*

Stuff a fish with potato and onion filling; put into a deep pan and bake. Put in separate pan a tablespoonful of lard or butter and as soon as hot put in two or three slices of onion. When onion is brown add one-half can of tomatoes, a cupful of hot water, salt and one tablespoonful of *Gebhardt's Eagle Chili Powder.* Cook for fifteen minutes, thicken with a little flour and pour over fish about ten minutes before serving.

Lobina Hervida ú Otro Pescado—*Boiled Bass or other Fish*

Put sufficient water in the pot to entirely cover the fish and season with one-half cupful of vinegar and onion cut fine, salt, pepper and a tablespoonful of *Gebhardt's Eagle Chili Powder.* Sew up fish in a piece of muslin or netting, fitting it to shape. Heat slowly for the first half hour, then boil, allowing about eight minutes for each pound of fish; unwrap the fish and pour over it a cupful of drawn butter, take liquor in which fish was boiled and add juice of one-half lemon, stirring in flour enough to thicken, and serve.

Fritada de Pescado—*Fried Fish*

A small fish should be cleaned, washed and drained, then well salted and rolled in Indian meal and flour that has been well mixed with a liberal dash of *Gebhardt's Eagle Chili Powder.* Fry in deep hot lard.

Camarón Estofado—*Stewed Shrimp*

One pint peeled shrimp; two tablespoonsful butter; two tablespoonsful tomatoes; one and one-half pints soup stock; two bay leaves; one-half teaspoonful minced parsley; one-half teaspoonful minced onion; one tablespoonful browned flour; one teaspoonful salt; one teaspoonful *Gebhardt's Eagle Chili Powder.* Heat butter, fry shrimp in it, then add flour, tomatoes, onion, stock, herbs and chili powder. Cook one hour.

Verduras
Vegetables

Tomate al Estilo Español—*Spanish Tomatoes*

Peel and slice one quart of tomatoes or use one three-pound can, removing seed. Cut in small pieces three bell peppers. Take four onions and boil until tender, then add tomatoes and pepper to the onions and simmer for one hour, season with salt, pepper and one tablespoonful of *Gebhardt's Eagle Chili Powder*, adding chili powder about one-half hour before done. Then prepare two cupsful of stale bread crumbs; mix alternately in a dish tomatoes and bread crumbs; moisten slightly with a little lard and sprinkle on each layer *Gebhardt's Eagle Chili Powder*, covering the top with bread crumbs, and bake in hot oven for ten or fifteen minutes.

Tomates y Chiles Verdes Rellenos, Etc.—*Stuffed Tomatoes, Green Peppers, Etc.*

Carefully select large tomatoes and take out the centers, fill with stuffing composed of soft bread crumbs, chopped parsley and a little lard, thoroughly mixing the whole with a teaspoonful or more of *Gebhardt's Eagle Chili Powder*, salt and pepper, and lay in a buttered baking-pan, baking in a hot oven about thirty minutes.

This recipe may also be used in preparing sweet green pepper, summer squash, onions and egg-plant, any of which make a most delightful dish. Rice may be used instead of bread crumbs if desired.

Berenjena—*Egg-Plant*

Peel the egg-plant and slice, drop in boiling water and boil ten minutes, then roll in flour mixed with one tablespoonful of *Gebhardt's Eagle Chili Powder*. Drop in a skillet full of boiling lard and fry to a delicate brown. Lay smoothly on a hot platter, sprinkle with salt and serve at once.

Guisado de Verduras—*Ragout of Vegetables*

Parboil one carrot, one turnip, two potatoes, two ears of corn, one cupful of lima beans and the same of peas, one onion and with them one-half pound of fat salt pork. Slice carrot, turnip, potatoes and onion.

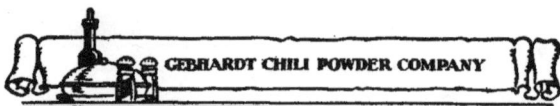

Put into a saucepan with a cupful of some good meat soup before it has been thickened and one tablespoonful of *Gebhardt's Eagle Chili Powder* and desired amount of salt. Cut the corn from the cob and add with the peas, beans and a sliced tomato as soon as the rest are hot. Stew altogether one-half hour. Stir in a large lump of butter; stew five minutes and serve in a deep dish.

Tomates Horneados—*Panned Tomatoes*

Select nice large tomatoes and cut them in halves, dip in flour and put the cut side down in a pan in which has been heated one or two tablespoonsful of butter. Then cook over a hot fire until brown; remove tomatoes to a hot dish and mix in the pan a sauce made of one tablespoonful of flour, one cupful of milk well mixed with one teaspoonful of *Gebhardt's Eagle Chili Powder* and one-half teaspoonful of salt. Boil for ten minutes and pour over tomatoes.

Arróz y Frijol Colorado—*Rice and Red Beans*

Soak for five or six hours (over night is better) a pound of beans and simmer them for at least four hours in two quarts of water until beans are soft. Add a teaspoonful of salt, a teaspoonful of butter or half lard and half butter, a small finely-chopped onion, one tablespoonful of *Gebhardt's Eagle Chili Powder* and let simmer for two hours longer; when about done add one cupful of well-cooked rice. A pound of salt meat can be substituted for the above seasoning, excepting the onion and chili powder, which add greatly to the taste of the dish.

Frijoles Cocidos en Horno—*Baked Beans*

Soak over night in cold water a quart of white beans, then put into fresh water and simmer until on removing a few and cooling in a spoon they burst slightly. Drain thoroughly and put into an earthen bean pot. Mix one level teaspoonful of salt with one-half cupful of molasses, add a little water and pour over the beans. Then bake from ten to twelve hours in a slow oven. When thoroughly baked add three or four tablespoonsful of lard and keep beans moist by adding hot water as needed until the last hour. When the last water is added put in one to three spoonsful of *Gebhardt's Eagle Chili Powder* and mix thoroughly.

Macarrón ó Fideos

Macaroni or Spaghetti

Sopa de Macarrón ó Fideo—*Boiled Macaroni or Spaghetti*

Break macaroni or spaghetti into two- or three-inch lengths and drop into large kettle filled with boiling salted water and boil as directed for rice, from thirty to thirty-five minutes; drain thoroughly in a colander, then pour cold water through the colander to remove the pastiness; reheat, add a little butter or tomato sauce and sufficient *Gebhardt's Eagle Chili Powder* to flavor thoroughly, and sprinkle over and through it grated cheese.

Macaroni cooked this way but without the cheese makes a very palatable addition to Chili Con Carne.

Tortas de Macarrón—*Macaroni Croquettes*

Break one-third of a package of macaroni and place in boiling salted water and cook for thirty minutes; then drain and chop finely. While doing this, bring to a boil one-half pint of milk, adding to it two tablespoonsful of flour and stir until a thick paste is formed. To this paste add one-half pound grated cheese and two tablespoonsful of *Gebhardt's Eagle Chili Powder* and the yolks of three eggs, mixing thoroughly; cook for a moment, then season to taste, add the macaroni and let cool; when cold form into croquettes, roll in cracker crumbs and fry in deep hot lard.

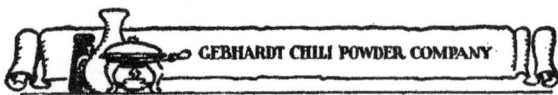

Sopa de Fideos—*Spaghetti*

Have two tablespoonsful of lard very hot in a frying-pan; add one-half button of mashed or minced garlic, then break spaghetti and add to lard; brown a little; add to it one sliced tomato; one-half sliced onion; a few grains of pepper and salt to taste; one teaspoonful of *Gebhardt's Eagle Chili Powder* and a little hot water; mix thoroughly and boil for about fifteen minutes. Serve while hot.

Macarrón Con Salsa de Hongo—*Macaroni with Mushroom Sauce*

Boil desired amount of macaroni in salt water; when done drain all water from it.

Make a cream sauce of butter size of an egg, two tablespoonsful of flour blended with it, salt to taste; add one pint of sweet milk, one can of small mushrooms, also half of the mushroom juice, four tablespoonsful of grated cheese, one tablespoonful of *Gebhardt's Eagle Chili Powder*.

Arróz Sazonado Con Chili—*Rice Seasoned with Chili*

Take one-half cupful of rice, rinse in cold water through sieve and put in a frying-pan with one or two buttons of garlic chopped fine and fry until slightly brown. Take one tomato and one onion cut into small pieces, mix with the rice, adding salt and pepper to taste and one-half teaspoonful of *Gebhardt's Eagle Chili Powder;* then add water and let steam or boil until done.

Ensaladas
Salads

Ensalada de Hígado Con Chili—*Liver Salad with Chili Dressing*

Use one-half pound of boiled liver chopped very fine; one tablespoonful of melted butter; a pinch of salt; a small finely chopped onion; one chopped hard-boiled egg and one heaping teaspoonful of *Gebhardt's Eagle Chili Powder*. Melt the butter and stir into it the *Eagle Chili Powder*, salt, onion and egg; when thoroughly mixed pour over the liver and serve on lettuce leaves with slices of hard-boiled egg on top.

Ensalada Mexicana—*Mexican Salad*

Cut three green sweet peppers and one small onion in a chopping-bowl; then add four ripe tomatoes, chop fine and season with salt, add and mix thoroughly one teaspoonful of *Gebhardt's Eagle Chili Powder* and pour in one-half cupful of vinegar and the grease from four or five slices of fried bacon.

Serve in small salad dishes. This makes a splendid relish for meats and vegetables.

Ensalada de Patatas—*Potato Salad*

Mix one tablespoonful of flour with one tablespoonful of melted butter or bacon grease; add one-half teaspoonful of salt; one heaping teaspoonful of *Gebhardt's Eagle Chili Powder* and one cupful of vinegar; boil and stir until smooth. Cut potatoes into small dice and add finely chopped onions to taste; then mix with the above dressing.

Ensalada de Tomate—*Tomato Salad*

Pare the tomatoes with a very sharp knife, slice and lay in the salad bowl. Make a dressing by thoroughly mixing one-half teaspoonful of salt with a teaspoonful of *Gebhardt's Eagle Chili Powder*, to which is added a drop at a time two tablespoonsful of olive oil. When thoroughly mixed put in one egg and four tablespoonsful of vinegar.

Ensalada de Repollo—*Cabbage Salad*

Take a small head of cabbage, chop very fine and let soak in vinegar until it becomes quite sour; then strain off most of the vinegar, sprinkle a little salt and one tablespoonful of sugar. Break five eggs in a pan of boiling water and add one-half teaspoonful of *Gebhardt's Eagle Chili Powder;* after eggs are done slice them and put them on the cabbage.

Ensalada Hecha de Carnes de Cerdo, Gallina ó Ternero — *Meat Salad made from Pork, Chicken or Veal*

Chop meat fine and boil until very tender. About ten or fifteen minutes before meat is done add two table-

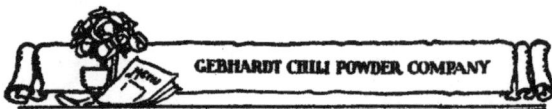

spoonsful of *Gebhardt's Eagle Chili Powder*. Have prepared six hard-boiled eggs, one onion, one teaspoonful of mustard, a bunch of celery, a bunch of parsley and one-half cup of melted butter; chop fine, pour in the melted butter and mix thoroughly. Garnish with slices of boiled eggs. A little lemon juice may be sprinkled over this if desired.

Ensalada de Combinación—*Combination Salad*

Use one cucumber, two young onions, three small radishes, four pieces of celery and two nice firm tomatoes, all cut in small pieces, and place in a salad-bowl, lined with lettuce leaves. Then prepare a dressing made of one-half cupful of vinegar, one tablespoonful of bacon grease or butter, one teaspoonful of salt and one tablespoonful of *Gebhardt's Eagle Chili Powder*. This dressing must be brought to a boil, then pour over the salad and serve.

Ensalada—*Salad Dressing*

Use the yolks of two hard-boiled eggs, rubbed very fine and smooth, one teaspoonful of English mustard, one teaspoonful of *Gebhardt's Eagle Chili Powder;* one teaspoonful of salt; the yolks of two raw eggs beaten together and a dessertspoonful of fine sugar; add to the above some fresh olive oil, poured in a little at a time, and beat as long as the mixture continues to thicken. Then boil one teaspoonful of *Gebhardt's Eagle Chili Powder* in one-half pint of vinegar for ten minutes and let cool. When the vinegar is cool, pour into the dressing, stirring constantly and adding additional vinegar until dressing begins to get thin.

Jalea de Tomate—*Tomato Jelly*

Cook one quart of tomatoes for ten minutes; add one teaspoonful of *Gebhardt's Eagle Chili Powder* and cook for ten minutes longer. When done add one-third package of gelatine and stir until it is soft; then strain and salt to taste and set away to cool. When the jelly is firm cut into small cubes, serving with mayonnaise dressing on lettuce leaves.

Caldos

Soups

Puchero de Familia—*Family Soup*

Take a small soup-bone with some fat, or three or
four quarts of the water in which mutton or soft beef
has been boiled, add to it bones from dressed meats,
trimmings of poultry, scraps of meat or beef gravy, a
couple of large onions, three tomatoes, one turnip, two
carrots and salt to taste. Set over a slow fire and let
simmer gently for about six hours. Remove all scum
as it rises. About thirty minutes before the soup is
done, stir thoroughly and add two tablespoonsful of
Gebhardt's Eagle Chili Powder; strain through a fine
sieve and serve.

Puchero de Pastas ó Verduras—*Soups with Pastes or Vegetables*

To a small soup-bone with some fat add vermicelli,
barley, rice or tapioca and vegetables and boil two
hours or until nearly done. Then add one tablespoonful of *Gebhardt's Eagle Chili Powder* for each quart of
soup and continue to cook for ten minutes and serve.

Caldo de Tomate—*Tomato Soup*

Use one can of tomatoes, one teaspoonful of salt,
one tablespoonful of sugar, five cloves, one tablespoonful of *Gebhardt's Eagle Chili Powder*, a pinch of black
pepper, one tablespoonful of finely chopped onions,
the same amount of chopped parsley and one pint of
water, stewing together for ten or fifteen minutes.
Then rub through a sieve, return to the fire and thicken
with a tablespoonful each of butter and flour rubbed
together.

Caldo de Cola de Rés—*Ox-tail Soup*

Cut one ox-tail into joints and fry to a brown in
good drippings. Slice three onions and four carrots
and fry in the same drippings, after you have taken
out the ox-tail. When done, tie some fine parsley in a
bag and drop into the soup-pot; put in the tail and add
to it about two pounds of lean beef, cut into strips,
grate over it two whole carrots, pour in about four
quarts of cold water and boil slowly for four hours;

GEBHARDT CHILI POWDER COMPANY

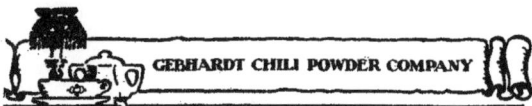

then strain, season with salt and pepper and thicken with brown flour wet with cold water; add one table-spoonful of *Gebhardt's Eagle Chili Powder*, boil fifteen or twenty minutes longer and serve.

Quingombo—*Gumbo*

Put in a big pot a large spoonful of lard, bring to a boil, then add a little flour, browning it slightly. To this add one large onion, one-half button of peeled garlic, both cut very fine. Then put in six large quartered crabs, two dozen fine sliced okra, one large cup of tomatoes, cut very fine, three or four sprigs of parsley, a couple of bay leaves, and, last of all, a pound of shrimp (about twenty). Let this stew together for twenty or twenty-five minutes, stirring constantly to avoid scorching. Then add two quarts of water and one and one-half to two tablespoonsful of *Gebhardt's Eagle Chili Powder*, stirring thoroughly as added and simmer for at least one hour. When done, add salt and pepper to taste, serving with a spoonful of boiled rice in each plate. If desired you may add to this, ham fried in lard and cut up fine, or a pound of finely cut veal.

Sopa de Migas—*Tortillas Soup*

Take some tortillas and cut in small pieces; drop them in a frying-pan where you have previously heated some lard. When slightly brown, add one button of garlic and onion chopped fine, one sliced red tomato (or five or six mashed green tomatoes), salt, pepper, one to one and one-half teaspoonsful of *Gebhardt's Eagle Chili Powder* and one-half teacupful of hot water; let boil for about ten minutes and then serve.

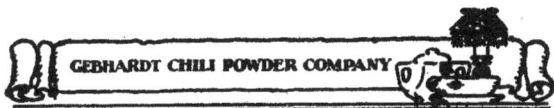

Recipés
Para la Preparación de Huevos
Egg Recipes

Tocino y Huevos Con Chili—*Bacon and Eggs with Chili Flavor*

Fry quickly thinly sliced lean breakfast bacon and when crisp take out of the frying-pan and keep hot; add to the grease remaining in the frying-pan a double sprinkle of *Gebhardt's Eagle Chili Powder* and heat to a boiling point. If there is not sufficient grease a tablespoonful of lard may be added. Break the eggs into the pan one at a time, sprinkle with pepper and a very little salt, removing eggs from frying-pan as soon as done.

The bacon will be improved if placed directly on ice for twenty or thirty minutes before frying.

Fritada de Huevos—*Omelet*

Break desired number of eggs in a bowl and beat until thoroughly mixed, adding with each egg a teaspoonful of cold water and one-fourth of a teaspoonful of *Gebhardt's Eagle Chili Powder;* when thoroughly mixed turn into a very hot frying-pan in which you have put one tablespoonful of butter, and cook until eggs begin to set; fold over and serve hot.

Fritada de Huevos Con Queso, Etc.—*Cheese and other Omelets*

The omelet is prepared as above and when it begins to set, sprinkle the center thickly with finely grated mild cheese. Fold over and serve on hot dishes.

Cooked meats, parsley, tomatoes, etc., may be added instead of cheese if desired.

Huevos Revueltos Con Chili — *Scrambled Eggs Flavored with Chili*

Break six eggs and add a tablespoonful of water and a liberal pinch of *Gebhardt's Eagle Chili Powder* for each egg; also salt and pepper to suit taste; beat lightly until whites and yolks are thoroughly mixed. Pour into a heated frying-pan brushed with lard or bacon grease and stir over the fire until thick and creamy. Serve on hot buttered toast.

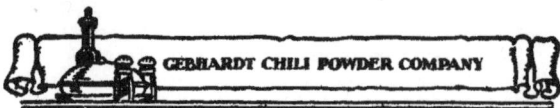

Huevos Horneados o Guisados—*Shirred or Baked Eggs*

Butter small stone-ware dishes and break into each, one egg, using care not to break the yolks; add a little butter and salt and sprinkle over the egg finely grated cheese, thoroughly mixed with *Gebhardt's Eagle Chili Powder*, using three parts of cheese and one part of chili powder; bake in an oven until thoroughly set.

Bread crumbs, chopped onions, parsnips, or stewed tomatoes may be substituted for the cheese or the chili powder alone may be sprinkled over the eggs.

Huevos Buñuelados—*Puffed Eggs*

Have at least one inch of hot lard in a frying-pan and carefully break into a separate bowl the desired number of eggs; season and sprinkle liberally with *Gebhardt's Eagle Chili Powder*. Hold the edge of the bowl close to the frying-pan and slip in the eggs, which will immediately puff up. Brown on both sides, lift out the eggs and serve at once.

Huevos al Estilo Español—*Spanish Eggs*

Heat a little olive oil in a frying-pan. Cut up the meat of one or two potatoes, some shallots, one green sweet pepper; chop very fine and add one-third of a teaspoonful of *Gebhardt's Eagle Chili Powder*. Break into this two eggs, season with salt and pepper, mix well and serve quickly.

Huevos al Estilo Caracas—*Caracas Eggs*

Take three eggs, two ounces of chipped dried beef and one-fourth pound of mild cheese; one small cupful of tomatoes, one teaspoonful of butter, one heaping teaspoonful of mustard and a pinch of salt. Put the butter in a frying-pan first, then add one-half teaspoonful of *Gebhardt's Eagle Chili Powder*, the mustard and salt, stirring thoroughly until smooth; add the tomatoes, cover and cook until done. When tomatoes are done, add the beef finely picked and the cheese well grated

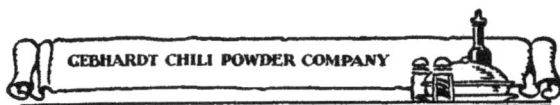

and the eggs which you have thoroughly beaten, stirring rapidly until smooth. Serve hot.

Huevos Con Queso—*Eggs with Cheese*

To six eggs use three tablespoonsful of grated mild cheese, one large tablespoonful of butter, one teaspoonful of onion juice or a small chopped onion; one-half teaspoonful of *Gebhardt's Eagle Chili Powder* and salt to taste. Mix the cheese, butter, onion, chili powder and salt in a hot pan and stir until cheese is melted. Break the eggs into a bowl, adding the cheese and cook slowly, stirring until done, and then stir in chopped parsley and serve hot.

Fritada de Huevos Española—*Spanish Omelet*

Make a plain egg omelet. For the sauce use one-half can of tomatoes, one onion, one green pepper, one tablespoonful of *Gebhardt's Eagle Chili Powder*, one tablespoonful of flour; salt to taste. Cut the onion in small cubes and saute in butter for several minutes; to that add *Gebhardt's Eagle Chili Powder*, salt and flour blended smoothly, tomatoes and green pepper; lastly boil for ten minutes.

Pour over omelet, roll and serve immediately. This sauce can also be used with noodles.

Viandas de Queso
Cheese Dishes

Tortas de Queso—*Cheese Balls*

With one cupful of grated cheese, mix thoroughly a teaspoonful of flour, one-half to one teaspoonful of *Gebhardt's Eagle Chili Powder* and one-half teaspoonful of salt; then stir in the stiffly beaten white of an egg, mold into balls and fry in deep hot lard.

Tostadas de Queso—*Cheese Toast (A Sunday-Night Supper)*

Mix one cupful of grated cheese with one-half to one teaspoonful of *Gebhardt's Eagle Chili Powder*, a

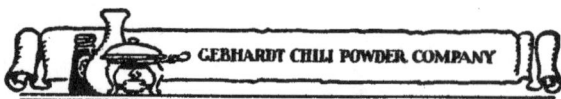

dash of salt and the beaten whites of three eggs; put on toast and brown in a quick oven.

Tiras de Queso—*Cheese Straws*

Sift one cupful of flour and mix four tablespoonsful of lard and stir with a fork. Add one cupful of grated cheese and a level teaspoonful of salt and one teaspoonful of *Gebhardt's Eagle Chili Powder*. Lastly add three tablespoonsful of ice water, roll on a flour-board about one-quarter inch thick, cut in narrow strips and bake in a quick oven.

Quesadilla Mexicana—*Mexican Rarebit*

Use one pound of rich, mild cheese grated, one tablespoonful of butter, one egg, one-half cupful of stale beer or milk if preferred, a pinch of salt and from one to two heaping tablespoonsful of *Gebhardt's Eagle Chili Powder*. First, put the butter in a sauce pan and when melted add the *Eagle Chili Powder* and salt, stirring until thoroughly mixed; add the cheese and continue to stir briskly until it is thoroughly melted; then slowly add the beer or milk, stirring all the time, and lastly add the egg and stir until the rarebit begins to thicken. Serve quickly on crackers or preferably on hot toast, being sure that your platters are hot.

Rellenos

Stuffings

Para Ternero, Cerdo ó Aves—*For Veal, Pork or Fowl*

To each cupful of dry bread crumbs salted to taste add a little oregano or sage and one-half teaspoonful of *Gebhardt's Eagle Chili Powder* and one tablespoonful of melted butter. To this may be added, if desired, a small chopped onion, a tablespoonful of mashed potatoes and one-half button of garlic chopped fine or a few raw oysters. When thoroughly mixed stuff the roast or fowl and bake or roast.

Enchiladas—

Take two pounds of Nixtamal or corn-meal, one teaspoonful of salt, one-half teaspoonful of *Gebhardt's*

32

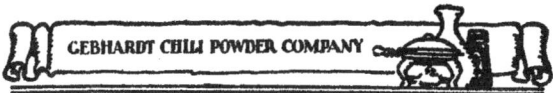

Eagle Chili Powder, or enough to color, and add sufficient water to make a thick dough, from which make thin cakes (similar to the ordinary corn cake) about 6 inches across. Have ready hot frying-pan in which you place two tablespoonsful of lard, from two to three tablespoonsful of *Gebhardt's Eagle Chili Powder*, a little salt and a little hot water; mix thoroughly and let boil for about ten or fifteen minutes, using sufficient water to prevent the mixture from getting thick; then put the cakes in just long enough to moisten both sides; remove and put on the cakes grated cheese and finely cut onions. Chopped olives and sardines cut into fine pieces are sometimes added. Then roll cakes and sprinkle over them grated cheese and finely chopped onions and serve quickly while hot.

Chiles Rellenos—*Stuffed Green Peppers*

A delightful stuffing for green peppers is made by preparing the meat the same as in Picadillo and adding raisins or nuts, such as pecans or English walnuts.

The peppers should be first scalded for a few moments, then skinned, seeded, stuffed and rolled in flour. Then dip in beaten eggs that have been salted and prepared to taste; fry and serve hot.

If preferred, peppers cooked in this way may be stuffed with cheese instead of meat and if a mild sharp cheese is used, they make a very appetizing dish.

Envueltos—

Take two pounds of Nixtamal or corn-meal, mix with sufficient water and make a thick dough and make into cakes about 6 inches across. Then take two pounds of beef or pork which has been boiled, and chop fine; have ready a hot frying-pan and put in two tablespoonsful of lard, from one-half to one button of garlic, mashed, one sliced onion; add the meat, salt and pepper to taste, one sliced medium-sized tomato and one teaspoonful of *Gebhardt's Eagle Chili Powder*. Mix thoroughly and let steam for about twenty minutes; add a little hot water or broth

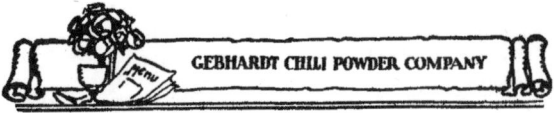

from the meat and when done add a small handful of raisins and pecans. Then place some of this filling on the cakes, which must be kept hot; roll over carefully, placing them on a hot platter, and cover the top with the filling or with gravy in which the filling has been cooked.

Serve while hot.

Salsas

Sauces, Catsups and Relishes

Salsa de Pescado—*Fish Sauce*

One-half teaspoonful of parsley; one tablespoonful butter; one tablespoonful flour; one-half pint soup stock; three or four tablespoonsful capers; one teaspoonful salt; one teaspoonful *Gebhardt's Eagle Chili Powder*. Heat butter, add flour, stock and seasoning and boil for ten minutes. When nearly done put in capers.

Salsa de Huevo Con Chili—*Egg Sauce with Chili*

Mash the yolks of two hard-boiled eggs, add oil and vinegar and season with salt and *Gebhardt's Eagle Chili Powder*. Mix the above thoroughly and sprinkle with finely cut parsley.

Salsa Italiana de Tomate Con Chili—*Italian Tomato Sauce with Chili*

Cook two tablespoonsful of chopped onions and one tablespoonful of butter until quite brown; then add about two tablespoonsful of flour, browning again, after which add one cupful of rich soup stock. To this add one-half can tomatoes that have been simmered for twenty minutes, with two cloves, two or three sprigs of parsley, one teaspoonful of fine herbs, one-half teaspoonful of allspice and one teaspoonful

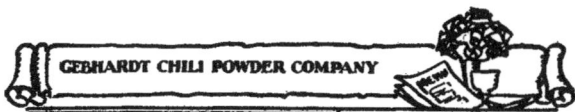

of *Gebhardt's Eagle Chili Powder*. Let the whole simmer for ten minutes longer and run through a sieve.

This makes a delightful sauce for chops, cutlets, etc.

Salsa Mexicana de Tomate—*Mexican Tomato Sauce*

Simmer one-half can of tomatoes, one chopped onion, a little cloves and one teaspoonful of *Gebhardt's Eagle Chili Powder*, together for ten minutes; season with salt and pepper to taste and rub through a sieve. Then cook together for one minute one tablespoonful of sifted flour; one tablespoonful of butter and slowly add the tomatoes, stirring until smooth, allowing the whole to simmer for about five minutes.

Salsa de Tomate Con Chili, Sencilla—*Plain Tomato Sauce with Chili*

Thoroughly mix one-half to two tablespoonsful of sifted flour with a like quantity of lard and cook for three or four minutes, stirring briskly; then add two cupsful of strained tomatoes, season with salt and pepper and a few drops of lemon juice and from one to three teaspoonsful of *Gebhardt's Eagle Chili Powder*, and cook from fifteen to twenty minutes until done. If desired a little sugar may be added to this.

Salsa para Gallina—*Chicken Gravy*

After cooking the fowl, pour off the extra fat in the pan, place the pan back on the stove and season with from one to two tablespoonsful of *Gebhardt's Eagle Chili Powder*. Add sufficient sifted flour to absorb the fat, stirring until well browned, and gradually add hot water or the chopped giblets with the water in which they have been cooked; continue to stir until smoothly thickened; then simmer for three minutes and serve.

Salsa de Chili—*Chili Gravy*

This may be made of any brown or meat gravy by adding to each one-half pint of gravy, one teaspoonful of *Gebhardt's Eagle Chili Powder*, stirring thoroughly and cooking for ten minutes. This makes a very rich sauce for fried eggs, cooked rice, baked beans, etc.

Salsa de Tomate Con Chili—*Tomato Catsup with Chili*

A very delightful flavor is imparted to this condiment by adding *Gebhardt's Eagle Chili Powder* to the tomatoes, onions and other spices commonly used.

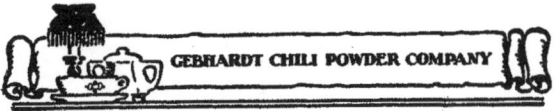

Salsa Mexicana—*Mexican Relish*

Use four green tomatoes, two green peppers, one onion, a very small bit of horseradish; chop the above together or grind very fine. Place this in a jar and cover with boiling vinegar, to which has been added a teaspoonful of salt and two tablespoonsful of *Gebhardt's Eagle Chili Powder* and one tablespoonful of mustard. The chili powder should be boiled in the vinegar for at least ten minutes before the seasoning is added. This is a delightful relish served with all meat dishes.

Salsa Española de Mostaza y Chili—*Spanish Chili Mustard*

Take three tablespoonsful of mustard, one tablespoonful of sugar, one egg (not separated); into this mix one cupful of vinegar and three tablespoonsful of *Gebhardt's Eagle Chili Powder*. Put into vessel containing cold water and boil for ten minutes, stirring constantly until thick. When cold add a tablespoonful of olive oil, and bottle.

Salsa de Chili—*Chili Relish*

Made from five pounds green tomatoes; three pounds white onions; three pounds cabbage; three tablespoonsful ground white mustard seed; three tablespoonsful ground allspice; four tablespoonsful of *Gebhardt's Eagle Chili Powder*, one teacupful fine sugar; one quart pure cider vinegar.

Place green tomatoes in chopping bowl and cover with one teacupful of salt, chop fine and as the green water rises pour it off. When chopped very fine squeeze in the hands and place in a large granite cooking vessel. Chop cabbage, add finely chopped onions and mix thoroughly; add celery seed, mustard seed, allspice, sugar and vinegar. Cook slowly for forty-five minutes then add four tablespoonsful of *Gebhardt's Eagle Chili Powder* and continue cooking for fifteen minutes

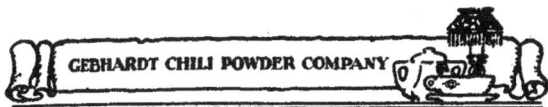

longer. When cold place in glass jars. This will keep in any climate and is a delicious relish for meats, fish, oysters, etc.

It also makes a delicate addition to cold lunches, which are very hard to put up in an appetizing manner.

Lonches

Sandwiches

Lonches Veracruzanos—*Vera Cruz Club Sandwich*

Between two slices of hot toast, place a crisp lettuce leaf, thin slices of turkey or chicken and thin slices of hot crisp bacon that have been sprinkled with *Gebhardt's Eagle Chili Powder* before frying and two slices of dill pickle. Then sprinkle well with *Gebhardt's Eagle Chili Powder* and a few drops of lemon juice or vinegar. Add a teaspoonful of olive oil and serve while hot.

Lonches de Chili—*Chili Sandwich*

Slice bread thin and butter. Lay between the slices crisp lettuce leaf and sprinkle well with *Gebhardt's Eagle Chili Powder* and a few drops of lemon juice.

Lonches de Jamon y Chili—*Ham and Chili Sandwich*

To one pound of boiled ham ground fine, add one minced onion and one tablespoonful of *Gebhardt's Eagle Chili Powder*, mixing thoroughly, and spread over thin slices of buttered bread.

Tortillas—*The National Bread of Mexico*

Take one quart of Nixtamal, mixing just enough water to make a thick dough, and bake on top of stove without grease. Shape the tortilla in the hands, as you would a corn pone, only making it not more than one-fourth of an inch thick and about 5 inches in diameter.

If Nixtamal cannot be secured a very good tortilla can be made from scalded cornmeal or, better still, from the whole corn. Where the whole corn is used, put one quart of corn into a pot full of water, add one and one-half tablespoonsful of lime and let boil over a good fire until soft, then cool and wash in clear water three or four times to remove the hull, and grind very fine.

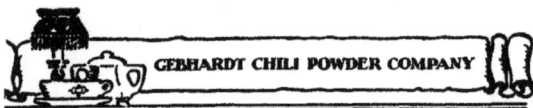

GEBHARDT CHILI POWDER COMPANY

Lonche Mexicano
Mexican Luncheon

Sopa de Tortillas
Tortillas Soup

Apio   Cebollas Adobadas
Celery   Pickled Onions

Ostras Angeles
Oyster Angels

Chili Con Carne, Gebhardt's "Aguila"
Gebhardt's Eagle Chili Con Carne

Jalea de Tomate
Tomato Jelly

Huevos Cremados
Shirred Eggs

Enchiladas   Tamales

Ensalada Mexicana
Mexican Salad

Tortillad

Cafe   Chocolate
Coffee   Chocolate

Comida Mexicana
Mexican Dinner

Cocktail de Ostras Con Salsa de Tabasco "Aguila"
Eagle Tabasco Oyster Cocktail

Caldo de Arroz y Verduras
Rice and Vegetable Soup

Fajada de Holibut Con Salsa
Halibut Steak with Sauce

Ensalada Mexicana, Mexican Relish

Gallina Frita Con Chile y Arroz
Fried Chicken with Chili and Rice

Chili Con Carne, Gebhardt's "Aguila"
Gebhardt's Eagle Chili Con Carne

Tomates Relienos   Berenjena Frita
Stuffed Tomatoes   Fried Egg-Plant

Macarron Con Salsa de Hongo
Macaroni with Mushroom Sauce

Tortillas

Ensalada de Combinacion, Combination Salad
Nieve, Ice Cream

Cafe   Chocolate
Coffee   Chocolate

Nueces Descortezadas, Shelled Pecans

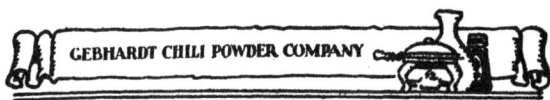

Index